W9-BAZ-951

PIONEERS OF SCIENCE

ARCHIMEDES

Peter Lafferty

The Bookwright Press
New York · 1991

Pioneers of Science

Archimedes
Alexander Graham Bell
Karl Benz
Marie Curie
Thomas Edison
Albert Einstein

Michael Faraday
Galileo
Guglielmo Marconi
Isaac Newton
Louis Pasteur
Leonardo da Vinci

First published in the
United States in 1991 by
The Bookwright Press
387 Park Avenue South
New York, NY 10016

First published in 1991 by
Wayland (Publishers) Limited
61 Western Road, Hove
East Sussex BN3 1JD, England

Library of Congress Cataloging-in-Publication Data
Lafferty, Peter.
    Archimedes / Peter Lafferty.
      p. cm. – (Pioneers of science)
    Includes bibliographical references and index.
    Summary: Examines the life, discoveries, and
contributions of the ancient Greek mathematician
who introduced mechanics, mathematical
formulas, and experimental science.
    ISBN 0–531–18403–X
    1. Archimedes – Juvenile literature. 2.
Mathematicians – Greece – Biography – Juvenile
literature. 3. Mathematics, Greek – Juvenile
literature. [1. Archimedes. 2. Mathematicians. 3.
Scientists.] I. Title. II. Series.
QA29.A7L34 1991
510'.92–dc20
[B]
[92]   90–21749
                                              CIP
                                               AC

Typeset by Kalligraphic Design Ltd, Horley, Surrey
Printed in Italy by Rotolito Lombardo S.p.A.

Contents

1 Archimedes' World

Archimedes was born over 2,000 years ago in the city of Syracuse on Sicily, an island near the "toe" of Italy. At that time, Syracuse was a Greek city, even though it was far away from the Greek mainland, for the civilization of Ancient Greece spread all through the eastern part of the Mediterranean region.

It was a Golden Age for Greece. Cities, such as Athens and Syracuse, were prosperous because traders came to them from all over the Mediterranean region. For many Greeks, this prosperity meant they had plenty of leisure time, which they liked to spend in thought and argument. Many new ideas began in the Greek schools and universities. The idea of democracy – that citizens should vote for their leaders – began in Greece.

The Greeks were also the first people to think logically about the natural world by looking for reasons for the things they saw about them. To them, it was not enough to explain natural events as the actions of their gods. This attitude led to the beginning of science as we know it today.

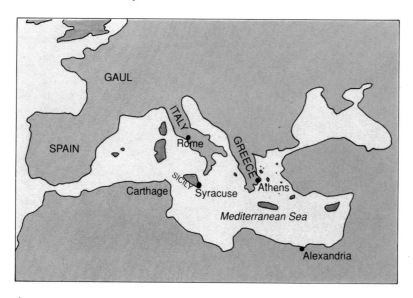

A map of the Mediterranean lands at the time of Archimedes. He was born and lived in the Greek city of Syracuse, in Sicily.

Before the Greeks, the Ancient Egyptians and Babylonians knew a little mathematics and astronomy. But these people did not try to explain what they saw about them. They were practical people: if they could use the movements of the stars to predict the best time to plant their crops, they were satisfied. It did not occur to them to investigate *why* the stars appeared to move. The Egyptians knew that a triangle with sides of 3, 4 and 5 units had a right angle in one corner, and they applied this to the design of their pyramids and buildings. However, it did not occur to them to wonder why such triangles had a right angle, or to wonder if

An Ancient Egyptian tomb painting of the harvest. The Egyptians used the movement of the stars to predict the best time to plant their crops.

5

other right-angled triangles were similar. It was left to a Greek scholar, Pythagoras, to discover that there is a connection between the lengths of the sides of a right-angled triangle. Pythagoras lived from about 570 to about 500 BC. His discovery is called Pythagoras'

Around 400 BC, the Greeks built a temple called the Parthenon in Athens. The goddess Athena was worshiped here.

theorem and is taught to children today. Pythagoras loved to study geometry, which is the mathematics of points, lines, angles, surfaces and solid shapes. He also loved to study numbers and do calculations. He thought that geometry and numbers were the key to understanding the natural world.

Other famous Greek scientists include Democritus, who lived from about 460 to about 370 BC. He suggested that everything is made up of tiny particles called atoms, but it took another 2,000 years before scientists were convinced that this was true.

Hippocrates, who lived from about 460 to about 377 BC, began the scientific study of medicine. One of his ideas was that a doctor should carefully study a sick person before prescribing treatment. This may seem obvious to us today, but in ancient times, when people thought that the gods caused diseases, this was a new idea.

The Babylonians, who lived in the country we now call Iraq about 2,600 years ago, were among the first astronomers. They thought that the Earth was at the center of a great globe surrounded by water.

Plato, who lived from about 427 to about 347 BC, was one of the greatest of the Greek thinkers. He taught the importance of logical thought and geometrical reasoning at his university in Athens. Aristotle, who lived from 384 until 322 BC, was Plato's pupil. He applied Plato's ideas to the study of the natural world.

However, the greatest scientist of Ancient Greece was Archimedes. He was born around 287 BC and died in 212 BC. Archimedes made many discoveries. He was an astronomer and built a model planetarium to show the way the stars and planets moved in the night sky. He estimated the distance from the Earth to the Sun and even calculated the number of sand grains required to

The Ancient Greeks painted scenes of everyday life on their vases. This vase from about 500 BC shows a young woman being adorned with jewelry.

The Ancient Greek thinker and scientist Aristotle, portrayed in a stone-chip, or mosaic, floor.

fill the entire universe! He was a skilled mathematician and proved many theorems in geometry. He found a way to calculate the area of a circle and the volume of a sphere, or ball shape. He studied how levers and pulleys worked and, using them, built machines capable of lifting huge weights. Some of his machines were used to defend Syracuse when it was attacked by the Romans in 215 BC.

9

This old picture shows Archimedes surrounded by some of his inventions.

Perhaps Archimedes' greatest discovery was to explain why objects float in water and other liquids. The reason is described in "Archimedes' Principle," which is still taught in schools today. A whole new science, called hydrostatics, which studies the forces found in still liquids, was started by his work on liquids.

Archimedes was the son of an astronomer and mathematician named Phidias. Not much is known about the early life of Archimedes or his family. It is probable that the family was a rich and noble one, perhaps related to Hieron, the King of Syracuse.

Like other Greek boys, Archimedes would have started school when he was eight years old. School was probably at the house of the teacher. In fine weather, the boys would sit on benches in the open courtyard of the house. The subjects taught would be familiar to children today: reading, writing, mathematics, music, and geography. Writing and calculations were done on a wooden board covered with wax. The letters were scratched in the wax using a sharp bone or iron stick. Older boys were allowed to write in ink on a roll of papyrus. Geometry problems were solved by drawing diagrams in wet sand on the floor.

This stone tablet from about 600 BC is carved with Greek letters. The writing describes how priests used the flight of birds to predict the future.

Although the Greeks were very interested in mathematics, they had a clumsy way of writing numbers. They used the letters of their alphabet as numbers. A mark next to a letter showed when it was being used as a number. Calculations with large numbers were very difficult because they had to have several marks to indicate their size. Another difficulty was that the Greeks had no number for zero. When he was older, Archimedes invented an easier way to write and calculate very large numbers.

α′	β′	γ′	δ′	ε′	ϛ′	ζ′	η′	θ′
1	2	3	4	5	6	7	8	9

ι′	κ′	λ′	μ′	ν′	ξ′	ο′	π′	ϙ′
10	20	30	40	50	60	70	80	90

ρ′	σ′	τ′	υ′	φ′	χ′	ψ′	ω′	λ′
100	200	300	400	500	600	700	800	900

```
   σ′μ′δ′        244
 + φ′π′η′        588 +
   ω′λ′β′        832
```

The first five letters of the Greek alphabet are called alpha, beta, gamma, delta, and epsilon. A small mark near a letter showed that it was being used as a number. Calculations, such as the one shown, were made the same way we do them, but calculations with large numbers were difficult.

When he had learned as much as he could from his teachers in Syracuse, Archimedes traveled to Egypt to study at Alexandria. This was the greatest city of the ancient world. It had been founded by Alexander the Great in 331 BC. There were many wonders for the young Archimedes to see. At the entrance to the harbor stood the famous Pharos lighthouse, several stories high, and with a bonfire at the top. It was one of the Seven Wonders of the ancient world. Another Wonder was the great museum and library of Alexandria, with more than a million books in the form of rolls of papyrus. The museum and library was like a university of today. The most learned men and women in the world were invited to work and teach there. They were paid a salary by the ruler, Ptolemy, and were free to devote themselves to research and study.

An old drawing of the Pharos lighthouse at Alexandria. Over 395 ft (120 m) high, it was built in 270 BC and was destroyed by earthquakes in AD 400.

One famous scholar who worked at Alexandria before Archimedes was born was Euclid. He lived from about 330 to about 275 BC. Euclid was a good mathematician but, perhaps more important, he collected, in a systematic way, all the geometrical results of Greek scholars. He arranged these results in a logical order and showed how complicated theorems could be proved from a small number of simple ideas. His book called *The Elements*, which showed how this could be done, was the most important geometry book in the world for over 2,000 years. Archimedes would certainly have studied it very carefully.

Archimedes' mathematics teacher at Alexandria, Conon, was also an astronomer. He studied the Sun's eclipses, but he is most famous for a piece of flattery. It is said that, in 245 BC, the King of Egypt was leaving for a battle. His queen, Bernice, cut off some of her hair and left it at a temple as an offering to the gods. The hair disappeared, perhaps stolen by souvenir hunters. However, Conon assured the Queen that the gods must have snatched the hair away because of its

The library at Alexandria was founded in 300 BC by the ruler of Egypt, Ptolemy; it was destroyed in AD 646 by Arab soldiers who conquered Egypt.

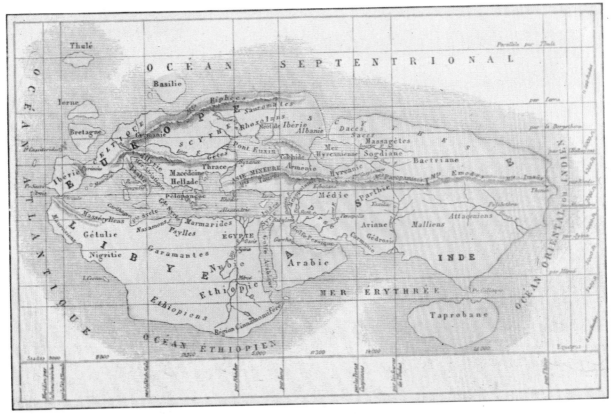

The following place labels appear on the map:

OCÉAN SEPTENTRIONAL · OCÉAN HYPERBORÉE · OCÉAN ATLANTIQUE · OCÉAN ÉTHIOPIEN · OCÉAN ORIENTAL ou INDIEN · MER ÉRYTHRÉE · Thulé · Basilie · Ierne · Bretagne · Ibérie · EUROPE · CELTIQUE · Germanie · SCYTHIE · Riphées · Sauromates · Rhoxolans · Albanie · Daces · Saces · Massagètes · Sogdiane · Bactriane · Mont Emodus · Mont Imaüs · Pont Euxin · Colchide · Hyrcaniens · Thrace · Macédoine · Hellade · Péloponèse · ASIE MINEURE · Arménie · Hyrcanie · Mont Paropamisus · Médie · Parthes · Ariane · Gédrosie · Carmanie · Malliens · Attagéniens · Crète · LIBYE · Marmarides · ÉGYPTE · Massésyliens · Gétulie · Nazamons · Psylles · Garamantes · Nigritie · Nubie · Arabie · INDE · Éthiopie · Éthiopiens · Région Cinnamomifère · Taprobane

beauty. He pointed to a dim group of stars and pronounced that they were the hair. Since then, that group of stars has been known as Coma Berenices, or "Bernice's Hair."

One of Archimedes' friends was called Eratosthenes. Like Conon, he lived most of his life at Alexandria, where he became chief librarian. He was a famous mathematician, astronomer and geographer. Julius Caesar consulted Eratosthenes' book on geography over a century after it was written. In mathematics, he devised a way of finding prime numbers – numbers that can be divided only by themselves – which is still known as the "sieve of Eratosthenes." Eratosthenes was also a poet and historian, and his nickname was "Beta," the second letter in the Greek alphabet. This was because he was the second most learned person in the world. Archimedes was nicknamed "Alpha," after the first letter in the alphabet, because he was the most knowledgeable person of his time.

Archimedes' method of finding the area of an irregular figure (geometrical shape). He used a balance arm to compare the figure with a known figure, such as a square or triangle.

Archimedes returned to Syracuse after his studies in Alexandria and settled down to a life of study and thought. He would sit for hours pondering geometry diagrams drawn in the sand floor of his house and often became so engrossed in a problem that he forgot to eat or to take care of himself. His servants had to persuade him to take a bath but, even in the bath, he drew diagrams on his wet skin.

Although he enjoyed geometry and mathematics most of all, Archimedes was also a practical scientist. He sometimes solved a geometry problem by doing an experiment, which is a test to see if an idea about the natural world is correct. An experiment uses real objects instead of words or diagrams. Today, all scientists test their ideas by doing experiments, but in Archimedes' time, most people believed that pure thought was the only way to make discoveries. Archimedes was one of the first scientists to do experiments.

Archimedes even had an experimental way of working out mathematical theorems. He called it his "method." For example, if he was trying to find the area of an irregular figure, or "geometrical shape," he would hang it on one end of a balance arm. On the other end of the arm, he would place a figure, such as a square, the area of which he knew. Then he would move the square until the arm was level and the figures balanced. He then measured the distance from the square to the center of the arm, and did the same for the unknown figure. If the unknown figure was twice as far from the center as the square, it was half the area.

In this way, Archimedes found that the area of a circle is the same as that of a triangle, when one side is equal to the circle's radius and the length of the base is equal to the distance around the circle, the circumference. Archimedes realized that his method did not really prove the theorem; it just gave a hint of the answer. He always tried to find an exact geometrical proof of any result obtained by his method.

Archimedes' practical abilities were put to good use by his friend King Hieron. In one case, the hold of a huge boat made for the King had become full of water

The Archimedean screw carries water upward as the inner spiral is turned. The screw is in fact a simple machine, since a small force on the handle can lift a large weight of water.

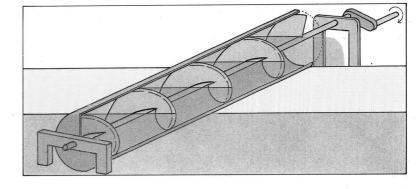

after a burst of heavy rainfall. No way could be found to remove the water from the boat, until Archimedes found the answer. He made a machine consisting of a hollow tube containing a spiral that could be turned by a handle at one end. When the lower end of the tube was put into the hold and the handle turned, water was

The Archimedean screw is still used today; here an Egyptian farmer uses one to irrigate a field.

carried up the tube and splashed out onto the ground next to the boat. These tubes – called Archimedean screws – soon became popular in Egypt, to lift water from canals for irrigation. They are still in use today. The screw is a simple kind of machine, and soon Archimedes was investigating other machines.

He found that the lever – another simple machine – could be used to raise up or shift heavy weights easily. A lever consists of a strong bar that rests on a stone, or other fixed object, which allows the bar to turn. If a heavy weight is placed on one side of the bar, close to the stone, a small force at the other end of the bar can lift the weight. "Give me a long enough lever," claimed Archimedes, "and I can move the Earth."

King Hieron thought Archimedes was exaggerating and set him a test using a large ship that lay aground

Archimedes is said to have boasted that he could move the Earth with a lever. Some versions of the story say that he also asked for somewhere to stand while working. This seems a sensible request, so the artist of this old drawing has obliged.

near Syracuse harbor. With three masts, and loaded with people and goods, it was so heavy that it could not be moved by an army of slaves. "Move the ship," he told Archimedes, "and I will believe your claim." But Archimedes decided to use the pulley, rather than the lever, for this "impossible" challenge. A pulley is a machine with a rope that runs over one or more grooved wheels set in a block. When the rope is pulled, the pulley magnifies the force to produce a larger force.

Archimedes moves a large ship, using a pulley. Such feats as this made Archimedes famous throughout the Greek world.

Types of levers

A lever is a simple machine. It consists of a strong bar rested on a support called the fulcrum. When the lever is pushed down at one end, it can lift a load at the other end.

There are three different types of levers. The first type has the fulcrum between the force, or effort, and the load. A crowbar is an example of this type of lever.

The second type of lever has the fulcrum at one end and the effort at the other end. The load is between the fulcrum and the effort. A wheelbarrow is an example of this type of lever.

The third type of lever has the fulcrum at one end and the load at the other end. The effort is applied between the fulcrum and the load. An excavator or digger is an example of this type of lever.

If a lever allows a small force to lift a large load, the lever is said to have a good or positive "mechanical advantage."

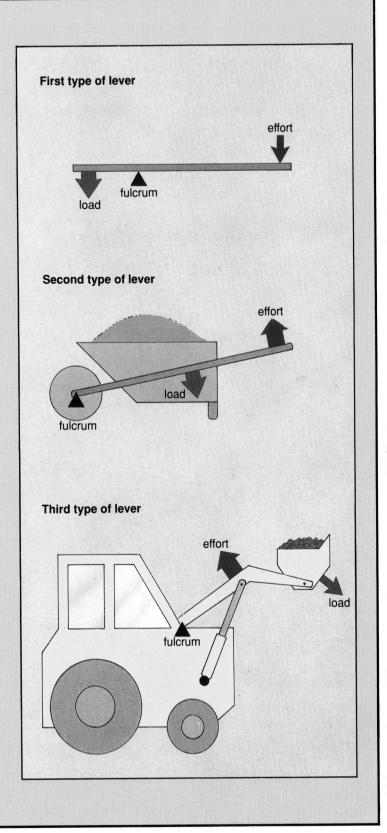

First type of lever

effort

fulcrum

load

Second type of lever

effort

load

fulcrum

Third type of lever

effort

load

fulcrum

21

Archimedes made a compound pulley – one with many wheels to greatly magnify the force – and tied one end of the rope to the ship. Imagine the King's astonishment when Archimedes, pulling the other end of the rope, easily dragged the ship into the water. With such demonstrations, Archimedes invented mechanics, the science of machines.

The pulley is a simple machine that enables a small force to lift a heavy weight.

4 King Hieron's Crown

One day, King Hieron set Archimedes a difficult problem to solve. He gave him a crown and asked, "Can you prove that this crown is pure gold, without damaging it, of course?" The goldsmith who had made the crown said that he had used all the gold that had been given to him. But King Hieron was suspicious – perhaps the goldsmith had taken some of the gold for himself and added silver to the crown to make it the correct weight.

An old picture of Archimedes in his bath, puzzling over King Hieron's crown.

Archimedes explains to King Hieron that his new crown is not pure gold.

Archimedes took the crown home and sat looking at it. What was he to do? He weighed the crown. He weighed a piece of pure gold just like the piece the goldsmith had been given. Sure enough, the crown weighed exactly the same as the gold. For many days, he puzzled over the crown. Then, one evening, while he was taking a bath, the answer came to him. His servants had filled the bath to the brim with water. As Archimedes lowered himself into the bath, the water overflowed onto the bathroom floor. Suddenly, he gave a shout and jumped from the bath. Forgetting that he was naked, he ran down the street to the palace, shouting, "Eureka!" In Greek, this means "I have found it." What Archimedes had realized was that when an object is placed in water it displaces an amount of water equal to its own volume.

To demonstrate his discovery he asked the King for a large jar filled to the brim with water, and set it in a bowl to catch any water that overflowed from the jar. Then Archimedes lowered the crown into the jar. Some water overflowed into the bowl. This was carefully caught and measured. Then the jar was refilled and the lump of gold lowered into the water. Once again water overflowed into the bowl. The amount of water was measured and, to the King's surprise, the gold had spilled less water than the crown. "King Hieron," said Archimedes, "this proves that the goldsmith has cheated. The crown and the gold both weighed the same so, if they were both pure gold, they would spill the same amount of water."

Archimedes explained that silver is lighter than gold, so, to make up the correct weight, extra silver was needed. This meant that the volume of the crown was slightly larger than the gold, so the crown spilled more water.

Later, Archimedes did more experiments by placing objects in water. He discovered that objects weighed

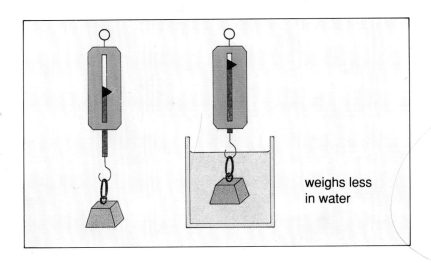

weighs less
in water

An object weighs less when in water than when in air. The water produces an upward force, called the buoyancy force, which supports the object.

The density of liquids

Archimedes found that the buoyancy force was greater in salt water than in pure water. This is because a volume of salt water is heavier than the same volume of pure water. Salt water is said to be more "dense" than pure water.

Archimedes made an instrument, called a hydrometer, to measure the "density" of a liquid (how much heavier a given volume of liquid is than an equal volume of pure water). It consisted of a thin rod, weighted at one end, which floated upright in a liquid. In a dense liquid, the stick floated with more of its length in the air than when it was in a less dense liquid. If a scale was marked on the stick, the density of liquids could be compared and measured.

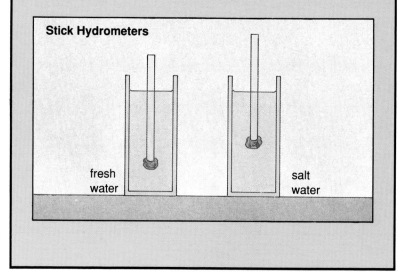

Stick Hydrometers

fresh water

salt water

less when they were placed in water or other liquids. There is an upward force, produced by the liquid, which supports the object. This upward force is called the buoyancy force. Furthermore, Archimedes found that the buoyancy force is always equal to the weight of the water or liquid that is displaced by the object. This was to become his most famous discovery. Nowadays, we know it as "Archimedes' Principle."

Archimedes could now understand why ships float even though they are heavy. A ship sinks down in the water, creating a buoyancy force big enough to cancel out its weight.

It is easy to float in the Dead Sea in Israel. The very salty water is so dense that there is a great buoyancy force.

Archimedes also found a way to measure the density of solid objects. He weighed the object in air, and then in water. By dividing the weight in air by how much weight the object lost in water, Archimedes found its density, or how much heavier the object is than an equal volume of water. He found that pure substances always have the same density, so he had a way of finding if a substance was pure. So, after all his experiments, he had found a second way to test King Hieron's crown: first to weigh the crown in air, and then in water. Next, to weigh some pure gold in air and water. If the crown were pure, it should lose the same proportion of its weight when in water.

Hot-air balloons float in air because the hot air inside them is not as dense as the cold air surrounding them. The cold air produces a buoyancy force that lifts the balloons.

5 ▼ Star Gazing

Astronomy is a very old science. Over 3,000 years ago, the Egyptians and Babylonians kept careful records of the stars they saw in the sky at each season. This helped them know when to plant their crops. The Egyptians also used the stars to lay out the pyramids in a north/south direction. Other peoples, such as the Chinese and Indians, were also interested in astronomy.

Ancient Egyptian priests observing the stars from a window in the Great Pyramid at Giza.

The Greeks were the first people to approach astronomy in a scientific way. About 450 BC, Anaxagoras of Athens suggested that the Sun was a red-hot rock larger than the Earth, and that the Moon reflected the Sun's light, like the Earth. These were new ideas, because most ancient peoples thought that the stars were gods.

The planets – star-like points of light that wandered among the stars – were named after the Roman gods. The smallest and swiftest-moving planet was called Mercury, after the messenger of the gods. The brightest was called Venus, after the goddess of beauty. The red planet was called Mars, after the god of war. Jupiter, the largest planet, was named after the king of the gods. Saturn, which moved only slowly, was named after the god who could make time stand still.

Observations of the planet Saturn made by Babylonian astronomers around 164 BC, recorded on a clay tablet.

An astronomer in Alexandria observing the stars. He is using a simple instrument to measure the angles and distances between stars. On the ground are models showing the position of the stars.

Around 400 BC, Eudoxus, a philosopher from the town of Cnidos on the coast of the country we now call Turkey, suggested that the planets were held in transparent spheres that moved around the Earth. Archimedes built a model planetarium to show how the planets moved. The model was made of glass spheres, one inside the other, and turned by water power. The Earth was at the center of the model, and each sphere held a small planet. As the spheres moved, the movements of the planets could be seen.

31

A statue of the Roman god Mars after whom the planet is named. Mars was the god of war.

Archimedes also made a device to estimate the size of the Sun. It consisted of a long rod or ruler with a small disk fastened at one end. The ruler was pointed at the Sun just as it was rising, since this was the only time it was safe to look at the Sun. The disk was moved along the ruler until it just hid the Sun. Archimedes was able to calculate the width or angle of the Sun by measuring how far the disk was along the ruler.

Calculating the Earth's circumference

Archimedes' friend Eratosthenes calculated the distance around the Earth. At midday in the middle of summer, the Sun was exactly overhead at Syene, a town about 497 miles (800 km) south of Alexandria. Seen from Alexandria at the same time, the Sun was seven degrees from the overhead point. Since a full circle contains 360 degrees and seven is about one-fiftieth of 360, Eratosthenes calculated that the distance around the Earth must be fifty times the distance from Alexandria to Syene, or about 24,850 miles (40,000 km). In fact, this is a remarkably accurate result. Modern measurements show that the Earth is about 25,000 miles (40,232 km) round.

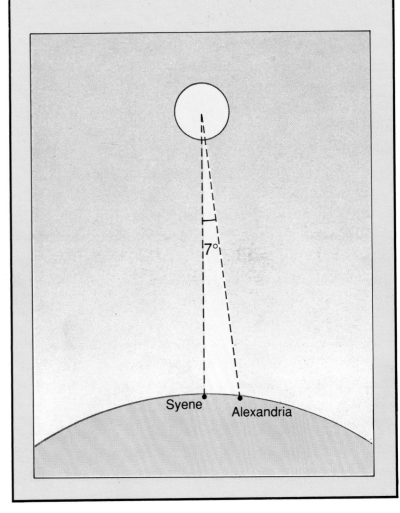

Archimedes calculated that the Sun was at least thirty times larger than the Moon. His calculation disagreed with that of Eudoxus, who thought that the Sun was nine times greater than the Moon. Phidias, Archimedes' father, had also estimated the size of the Sun. He concluded that the Sun was twelve times larger than the Moon. In fact, all these estimates are very wrong; the Sun is 64 million times larger than the Moon. You might, at first, be scornful of these poor results. However, it must be remembered that Greek astronomers had no instruments, such as telescopes, to help them.

Eratosthenes, Archimedes' friend at Alexandria, calculated that the distance around the Earth must be about 24,850 miles (40,000 km). Archimedes used this result to undertake a remarkable calculation. He wanted to prove to his fellow Greeks that it was possible to calculate with very large numbers. You will remember that Greek numbers were clumsy for large calculations. So Archimedes devised a new kind of number, called order numbers, which are written in the same way that scientists write large numbers today. Then Archimedes set out to calculate how many grains of sand it would take to fill the entire universe. He started by calculating how many grains would fit into the Earth. Then he calculated how many times the Earth would fit into the Sun. Next he calculated how many Suns would fit into the planet spheres of his planetarium. Then he multiplied this by 10,000 because he said that the sphere holding the stars was 10,000 times bigger than that holding the planets. At the end of his calculation, he found a huge number. We would write it as ten followed by sixty-three zeros. However, since the Greeks had no number for zero, Archimedes had to write the number down in words.

These calculations were important because it showed that numbers can be as large as we like and, no matter how large the numbers are, we can still do calculations with them.

Opposite In this planetarium, or model of the solar system, the Egyptian astronomer Ptolemy is turning a handle that moves the planets around the Earth. Ptolemy, who lived from AD 100 to 178, developed Aristotle's idea that the Earth is the center of the universe, with the Sun, Moon and stars revolving around it. It was not until 1543 that the Polish astronomer Nicolaus Copernicus showed that the Earth and other planets moved around the Sun.

Archimedes and Mathematics

More than anything else, Archimedes loved mathematics, especially geometry. He liked to study the shape of curves, to calculate the area inside curves and the volume of solid objects.

He discovered how to calculate the area inside a circle accurately. The ancient Egyptians had a rough way of doing this. They drew a large square outside the circle and a smaller square inside the circle. Then they calculated the area of each square; the area of the circle was somewhere between the two areas. Archimedes used the same idea, except that he drew polygons, or many-sided figures, inside and outside the circle. His polygons had 96 sides, so their sides were very close to the edge of the circle. He found that the distance around a circle, the circumference, was always about $3\frac{1}{7}$ times the distance across the circle, the diameter.

We use the Greek letter pi, or π, for this number, which is the ratio of the circumference of a circle to its diameter. The value we use for pi today is 3.14159...

To calculate the area of a circle, the Egyptians drew a square inside and outside the circle. The area of the circle was in between the areas of the squares (left). Archimedes improved on this by drawing many-sided figures (polygons) inside and outside the circle (right).

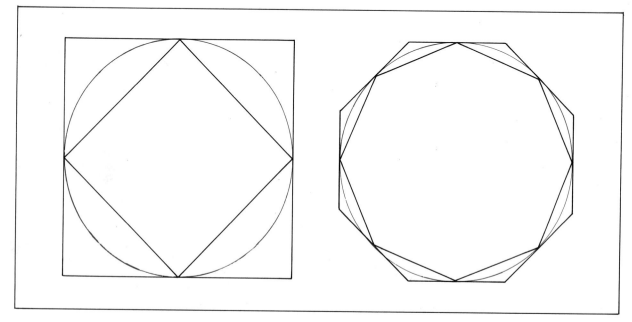

The area of a circle

The number pi is the distance around a circle (its circumference) divided by the distance across the circle (its diameter). This number is the same for all circles, 3.14159 . . . or about 22/7. Whatever the size of a circle, the distance around it is always just over three times the distance across it.

To find the area of a circle, you first find the radius of the circle. The radius is the distance from the center to the edge of a circle. The radius is half the diameter.

If you have a circle with a radius of 2 in, you find the area by first multiplying the radius by itself. This gives 2 in multiply 2 in = 4 sq in. Finally, you multiply 4 sq in by pi. So the area is 4 sq in x 22/7 = 12.57 sq in.

In algebra, this calculation is written:

Area = πr^2

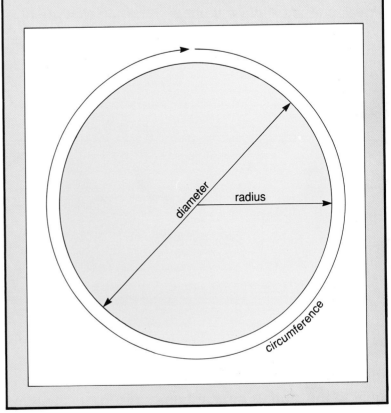

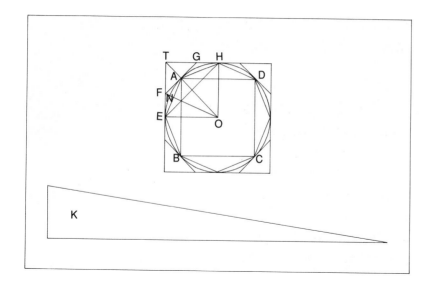

(the dots indicate that the string of numbers goes on forever). Archimedes found that pi lies somewhere between 3.1405 and 3.1428, which is quite accurate. (Today, mathematicians like to calculate the value of pi more and more accurately. It has now been calculated by computer to 480 million decimal places!) But Archimedes lived long before the decimal way of writing numbers was invented, so he had to write pi as a fraction.

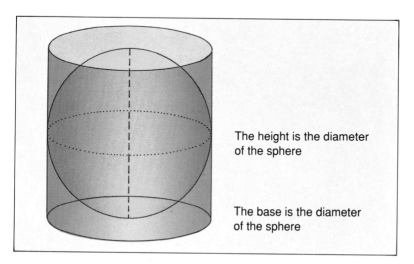

The height is the diameter of the sphere

The base is the diameter of the sphere

Archimedes proved that a sphere is two-thirds the volume of a cylinder when the height and width of the cylinder is the same as the width of the sphere.

Archimedes had proved that the area of a circle is the same as the area of a right-angled triangle, when one side is equal to the circle's radius and one other side is equal to the circle's circumference. From this and his work on pi, he deduced the formula for the area of a circle. It is the formula we use today:

Area of circle $= \pi r^2$

Archimedes also studied the sphere. He was able to show that the surface area of a sphere is four times the area of a circle drawn through the middle of the sphere. He also proved that the volume of a sphere is two-thirds of the volume of a cylinder drawn around the sphere, with the same width and height as the sphere. This result pleased Archimedes so much that he gave instructions that the diagram used in his proof was to

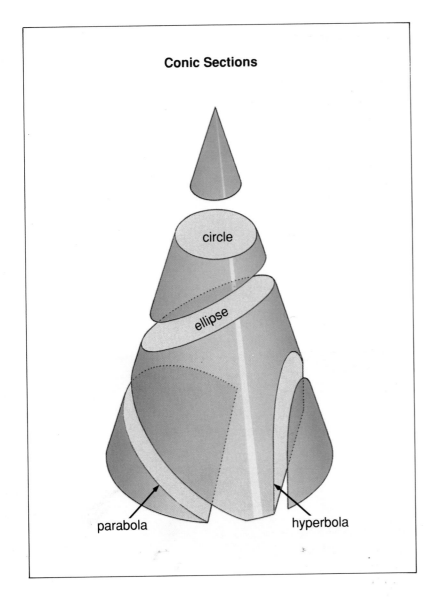

Conic Sections

circle

ellipse

parabola

hyperbola

Archimedes studied curves called the ellipse, hyperbola and parabola. These curves are called conic sections because, if you slice through a cone, you produce the curves.

be engraved on his tomb. He then went on to discover the formula for the volume of a sphere:

Volume of sphere = $\frac{4}{3} \pi r^3$

Archimedes also loved calculating with numbers. One day, he set a problem for his fellow scholars to solve. The problem was:

The Sun has a herd of bulls and cows. Some are white, some are gray, some are brown, and some are spotted. The number of spotted bulls is less than the number of white bulls by $\frac{5}{6}$ of the number of gray bulls. The number of spotted bulls is less than the number of gray bulls by $\frac{9}{20}$ of the number of brown bulls. The number of spotted bulls is less than the number of brown bulls by $\frac{13}{42}$ of the number of white bulls. The number of white cows is $\frac{7}{12}$ of the number of all the gray cows and bulls together. The number of gray cows is $\frac{9}{20}$ of the number of brown cows and bulls. The number of brown cows is $\frac{11}{30}$ of the number of spotted cows and bulls. The number of spotted cows is $\frac{13}{42}$ of the number of white cows and bulls. How many cows and bulls of each color?

This is a very complicated puzzle. You will need to be very good at algebra to solve it. The Greeks did not know any algebra, so Archimedes' friends must have had a hard time trying to solve the puzzle. There are a number of right answers or, in other words, the answer is "indeterminate." The smallest answer is:

spotted bulls = 4,149,387
white bulls = 10,366,482
brown bulls = 4,149,387
gray bulls = 7,460,514
spotted cows = 5,439,213
white cows = 7,206,360
brown cows = 3,515,820
gray cows = 4,893,246

Archimedes is said to have given a solution in which each number is 80 times larger than these.

7 ▼ The Siege of Syracuse

King Hieron died in the year 216 BC. The new King, Hippocrates, formed an alliance with Carthage, a great city on the coast of Africa in the country we now call Tunisia. Carthage was the enemy of Rome, the other great power in the Mediterranean region. The Romans decided to invade Syracuse and install a king who would be more friendly.

A famous general named Marcellus was in charge of the invasion. He set forth with a huge force of soldiers and a fleet of sixty quinquiremes – ships rowed by five rows of oarsmen on each side. They had huge catapults to hurl boulders into the city. An enormous war machine, called a *sambuca*, was built. It consisted of a huge ladder mounted on wheels with a bridge at the top that could be thrown onto the walls of the city. The

Marcellus, the Roman general who attacked Syracuse in 212 BC.

A Roman onager, a device for hurling stones great distances.

sambuca was so big that it had to be carried on the decks of eight ships chained together. Marcellus was confident that he would take Syracuse easily, but he had not reckoned on confronting Archimedes.

Archimedes is said to have placed huge curved mirrors on top of the city wall, and when the Roman fleet came in sight the mirrors were turned to focus the Sun's rays onto the ships. The heat was so great that many ships burst into flames. Other ships were destroyed by huge boulders thrown by the catapults built by Archimedes.

The Roman historian, Plutarch, described what happened to the *sambuca*: "While it was approaching the city walls, there was discharged at it a piece of rock of great weight, then a second and a third, which striking upon it with an immense force and a noise like thunder, broke all its foundation to pieces, shook out all its fastenings, and completely dislodged it, and it fell in pieces into the sea."

Any ships that came near the city were grabbed by iron hooks and lifted from the water using huge levers, and then dropped back into the sea from a great height. After a while, Marcellus saw that his attack had failed and withdrew to a safe distance. "We cannot continue to fight this geometrical Briareus, who plays pitch-and-toss with our ships and, with the multitude of darts that he showers at a single moment upon us, really outdoes the hundred-handed giants of mythology," he said. In Greek mythology Briareus was a giant with a hundred arms.

According to some stories, Archimedes used large mirrors to focus the Sun's rays onto Roman ships.

Marcellus decided to lay siege to the city. Syracuse was surrounded and no supplies were allowed in or out. The siege lasted three years. Eventually the Romans took advantage of an unguarded section of the city walls, and entered the city.

Archimedes was working on a mathematical problem when a soldier burst through the door. Not realizing that the city had been invaded, Archimedes ordered, "Go away, let me finish my work." The soldier, who did not recognize the famous man, drew his sword and killed him. When Marcellus heard of Archimedes' death he was heartbroken. He had given orders that Archimedes was not to be killed, but now it was too late. All that could be done was to bury Archimedes with great ceremony and honor. His tombstone was, as he wished, engraved with the geometrical diagram showing a sphere inside a cylinder, to remind the world of his discoveries.

Archimedes' crow was a giant "arm" said to have been used during the defense of Syracuse to overturn attacking ships. The engraving shows three of these "arms" defending the city.

A mosaic floor showing the death of Archimedes.

Archimedes hoped that his work would help the scholars who came after him. In particular, he hoped that his "method" of discovering geometrical theorems would be useful. Unfortunately, details of his method were lost for many years, so it had little influence on later scholars. However, the theorems he discovered are still important – formulas giving the area of a circle and the volume of a sphere and the value of pi, for example. Also, his procedure for calculating the area of a figure was adopted by modern mathematicians; it became part of "calculus," a branch of mathematics often used by scientists.

Many of the stories about Archimedes' machines are hardly believable, but the "law of the lever," pulleys as well as the Archimedean screw are all still used today. And, of course, everyone at school learns about "Archimedes' Principle," and how this explains why objects float in liquids.

45

Date Chart

About 570–500 BC Pythagoras teaches that numbers and geometry are the key to understanding the universe.

About 500–428 BC Anaxagoras proposes that the Sun is a red-hot rock larger than the Earth, and the Moon reflects the Sun's light, like the Earth.

About 460–370 BC Democritus suggests that everything is made up of tiny particles called atoms.

About 460–377 BC Hippocrates begins the scientific study of medicine.

About 427–347 BC Plato, the greatest of the Greek philosophers, teaches the importance of logical thought and geometrical reasoning.

About 408–355 BC Eudoxus suggests that the planets are suspended in moving crystal spheres rotating around the Earth.

384–322 BC Aristotle, Plato's pupil, begins the scientific study of the natural world.

About 310–230 BC Aristarchus realizes that the Sun is larger than the Earth. He also teaches that the Earth moves around the Sun. (This idea was not generally accepted by Greek scientists, but the Polish astronomer Nicolaus Copernicus revived it in 1543, and it was acknowledged by the Italian Galileo, although it was again not accepted.)

About 300 BC Euclid writes his book on geometry, *The Elements*, which is still used today.

About 287–212 BC Archimedes studies geometry, mathematics, hydrostatics, mechanics and astronomy.

273–192 BC Eratosthenes measures the Earth's size and maps the known world.

About 140 BC Hipparchus studies planetary movements, makes an accurate star map and estimates the distance to the Sun.

AD 127–148 Claudius Ptolemy sums up Greek astronomy, including the idea that the Sun moves around the Earth.

Picture Acknowledgements

Mary Evans 7, 10, 15, 41, 43; Michael Holford 5, 8, 11; Mansell Collection *cover*, iii, 13, 14, 20, 24; Ann Ronan Picture Library 19, 23, 29, 31, 42, 44; Ronald Sheridan's Photo Library 9, 18 (John Stevens), 30, 32, 45; Topham 35; Wayland Picture Library 6; Zefa 22, 27, 28. Illustrations by Jenny Hughes. Cover artwork by Richard Hook.

Glossary

Algebra   A kind of mathematics that uses symbols for unknown numbers.

Astronomy   The science that studies the stars, planets and other objects seen in the night sky.

Atom   The smallest part of a substance.

Buoyancy   The force that holds up a floating object.

Circumference   The distance around a circle.

Density   The "compactness" of a material, or the weight or mass of a substance in relation to its volume.

Diameter   The distance across the middle of a circle.

Displace   To move out of place.

Eclipse   When one body in space blocks the light of another body in space. A solar eclipse occurs when the Moon temporarily blocks out the light of the Sun.

Experiment   A test done in a laboratory to see if a scientific idea is correct, or to discover new facts.

Figure   A geometrical shape.

Geometry   A branch of mathematics that studies lines, angles, surfaces and solid shapes.

Hydrometer   An instrument for measuring the density of liquids.

Hydrostatics   The science that studies liquids at rest, in a tank or dam, for example.

Lever   A machine used for lifting heavy weights. It consists of a strong bar that turns about a fixed point, or pivot, like a seesaw.

Mathematics   The science that studies numbers and how they can be used in calculations. It includes arithmetic, algebra and geometry.

Mechanics   The science that studies how machines work.

Papyrus   A type of paper made by the ancient Egyptians from the stems of reeds.

Planet   A large body that moves around the Sun. The ancient Greeks knew about only five of the planets, Mercury, Venus, Mars, Jupiter, Saturn, and they thought the planets moved around the Earth.

Polygon   A figure with many sides.

Prime number   A number that can be divided only by itself and 1.

Pulley   A tool for lifting weights. It consists of a wheel with a groove around the rim in which a rope runs.

Research   Investigations into unsolved problems.

Sphere   A ball-shaped solid.

Theorem   A formula or statement in mathematics that can be deduced from other theorems.

Volume   The amount of space taken up by something.

Books to Read

Archimedes: Greatest Scientist of the Ancient World, D. C. Ibsen (Enslow Pubs., 1989)

Ancient Greek History, G. Polyzoides (Divry, 1980)

The Golden Days of Greece, Oliver Coolidge (Harper, 1968)

The Greek World, Anton Powell (Watts, 1987)

Greece 1600 – 30 B.C., Anton Powell (Watts, 1987)

Index